God probably doesn't exist

Patrick Lindenfors
Vanja Schelin

A book about not believing in Gods

Original edition *Gud finns nog inte* published by Fri Tanke förlag 2008

© Patrick Lindenfors 2008, 2011, 2014
© Illustrations Vanja Schelin 2008, 2011, 2014
Translation Patrick Lindenfors
Editor Christer Sturmark

ISBN 978-15-00227-86-9

Contents

To my children.

What does it mean to not believe in Gods?

All those Gods

Some people believe in a man in heaven who can do whatever he wants.

Others believe in a woman in heaven, or several men and women together. They have names such as Jehovah, Thor, Isis, Allah, Zeus, or Kali and they are called *Gods*.

There are also those who believe that God is an invisible force that sees and hears everything. Or that God is love.

But it is also perfectly possible not to believe in any of all those Gods.

This book is about not believing in God.

In the beginning no Gods existed

The first humans on earth were like all other animals and saw the world in the same way as all other animals see the world.

But the human brain evolved and made us able to think about things we don't see. We learned to plan and fantasise, tell stories and understand what would happen if we did one thing instead of another.

Then one day perhaps someone had a hard time keeping reality and fantasy separate. Or maybe one person boasted that he had a magic force on his side.

The first person to invent a God, at the same time made everyone else into non-believers.

It is still that way; everyone is born a non-believer. To believe in a God is something that you have to learn. The person who teaches you determines what God you will believe in. (If you don't invent a God for yourself.)

But you can also say "I don't believe in *any* Gods".

To not believe is not to believe

Some people say that it as much a belief to *not* believe in Gods as it is to believe in Gods.

But that can't be right? It isn't as much a belief *not* to believe in trolls as it is to believe in trolls or to *not* believe in unicorns as to believe in unicorns.

Just because someone invented a God, doesn't make everyone else equally much believers.

That is as strange as to say that *not* playing football is just as much a sport as it is to play football.

All people are non-believers

It is hard today to find people who believe that old Gods such as Thor, Zeus or Ra exist for real.

Many people in the Western world believe in the God of Christianity. People who live in India usually instead believe in several other Gods. Those people are called Hindus.

Those who believe in the Christian God seldom also believe in the Hindu Gods. So they are non-believers when it comes to the Hindu Gods.

No one believes in *all* Gods. (No one even knows the names of all Gods.) Most people believe in *almost no* Gods.

People who do not believe in any Gods just add one more God to the list of Gods they don't believe in.

Do you believe in fairies and gnomes?

Many things exist only in peoples' imagination. For example fairies in the garden or gnomes inside your calculator who do all the calculations.

Maybe you have stopped believing in Santa Claus? You probably never believed in trolls.

It is a good idea to think about why you believe in some things but not in others.

Don't believe anything that you don't have a good reason to believe!

This applies even to Gods.

Why write a book about not believing in Gods?

There are no special books written about not believing in trolls. If you invent a fantasy character of your own, no one will write a book saying that it is not for real. So why is it something special not believing in gods?

Probably because it is so common to believe that there exist gods of some kind. Many people around the world believe in gods. But only because a lot of people believe in something does not mean that it is true.

A long time ago many people believed that the earth is flat.

But it isn't.

Tales about reality

There are many tales of how Gods created the world. Some of them are collected in books such as the Bible and the Koran.

People who do not believe in Gods do not believe that any of these stories are true. Instead, many non-believers are curious about how the world works for real. That doesn't mean non-believers do not like tales and stories — only that they don't believe the stories are true.

Scientists today have concluded that the universe began almost 14 billion years ago. The material that the earth and we people are made of was created in stars that later exploded.

You are made of stardust!

Life on earth began about four billion years ago. After that, life has evolved into all the animals and plants that we can see today.

Everything that lives on earth is related!

Who needs made-up stories when reality is that fantastic?

(But how do we know that reality is real? That is a difficult question demanding a long answer; about as long as this book. Briefly, reality is what we can show each other. It is possible to show someone how we know when the universe began and how we know that everything that lives is related. But it is impossible to show someone paradise, or gods.)

The world's three largest religions

Christianity

Those who call themselves Christians believe in one God and that God sent his son down to earth. The son, whose name was Jesus, was also God. Since Christians only believe in one God, the Christian God must have sent himself down to earth as Jesus.

Christians say that Jesus' mother was Mary, a virgin made pregnant by God through an angel. Jesus could do fantastic things such as walking on water, healing sick people by only touching them, making water into wine, resurrecting dead people and making some fish and bread last enough to satisfy a whole crowd.

Jesus was nailed to a cross and died, but he became alive again after three days and flew to heaven.

That Jesus came to earth, was crucified, died and became alive was God's way of saying "I forgive you".

Christians believe that Jesus will come back to earth to judge the living and the dead. Those who believed that Jesus was God will live on in paradise. Those who believed that Jesus was an ordinary human, or perhaps didn't even exist, will burn forever in hell; even if they were good people when they lived.

Islam

Those who call themselves Muslims believe in a God whom they call Allah (which means "God" in Arabic) and that Muhammad was Allah's last messenger.

Muslims also believe that the angel Gabriel flew down to Muhammad on earth to give Allah's last message to humanity. Mohammad spoke to Gabriel alone in a cave. He remembered what Gabriel said and told it to others. This message was later collected in the book called the Koran.

Muslims therefore believe that the Koran contains the words of Allah himself.

Besides the Koran, many Muslims feel that it is important to follow something called *hadith*. These are tales of what Muhammad said and did. According to hadith, people who were once Muslims but then stop believing in Allah should be beheaded.

Some Muslims think that it is very important that women don't show their hair.

Hinduism

Most people who call themselves Hindus believe in a lot of Gods. They also believe that our souls existed in other bodies before we were born and that our souls move on to other bodies when we die.

You don't have to be reborn as a human, but can be reborn as an animal. If you behave really badly, you can become reborn as a fly.

If you behave really, really well, your reward is *not* to be born again.

What you do in one life determines what happens to you in the next. Because of this, disabled people – according to some Hindus – deserve to be disabled; it is their own fault.

Three important Hindu Gods are Brahma, Vishnu and Shiva. Brahma created the universe, Vishnu preserves it, and Shiva's role is to destroy it.

To choose a religion

There are many more religions in the world. They are all too many to describe in a book about non-belief.

Christianity and Islam both state that they teach the Only Truth and that all other religions are false. Hinduism claims that there are many truths, but that you are definitely reborn when you die.

All can't be right at the same time.

There is no way to find out which religion is true or false without dying first. How else can you find out if Jesus was God's son, Muhammad Allah's last prophet, or if you will be reborn as a donkey?

The problem is that if one religion is true, then the others must be false. You don't have to be a non-believer to understand that — the religions say so themselves.

Why does anyone believe in Gods?

Don't know

If you ask some people why they believe in a God they say "I don't know. Leave me alone."

But that is not a really good reason to believe in Gods. It is probably mostly an excuse for not having to think.

Another version of this is to say "It is not what you believe that is important, it is the rituals." But if what you believe is unimportant, then religions are not really needed, are they? You can make up any rituals you like anyway; squashing tomatoes with your toes, for example.

God as the first explanation

Nothing happens without a cause. A stone does not begin to fly by itself. But someone can pick up the stone and throw it. Then there is a cause that the stone flies.

If you follow all such causes back through time you should eventually come back to the place where it *all* began; the reason that the universe exists.

Some people call this first cause "God".

But it solves nothing to say that a God is the first cause. Because if *everything* needs a cause, then so does God. So what caused God?

If God doesn't need a cause, then *everything* does not need a cause. Maybe not even the universe?

Those who believe in God think that God is an exception, that he doesn't need a cause. But then you can make up anything you want to and say that *this* doesn't need a cause. Maybe a bored troll was the reason that it all began?

Instead, it is probable that everything doesn't need a cause.

God as an old explanation

Once, Gods were the best explanation of many things.

One could say "It rains because God wants it to". Today we know that rain is vapour that has become water again and falls down to earth as drops.

The more we have understood how the world works, the less we have had to use Gods as an explanation.

There are still those who believe in Gods because they think that this provides good explanations for how the world works. But now we have better explanations.

God as an excuse

Some people say that God is the explanation of the world's unsolved mysteries. Often they just say "the Gods willed it so", or "God created the world that way", and then they are done.

It is strange that someone is satisfied with that answer, because it is not really an explanation since God could just as well have done the opposite. You are surely left still wondering why it turned out one way and not the other.

What if you asked your parents why you can't stay out with your friends and they answered "Because". Would you be satisfied with that answer?

God as "whatever"

If you ask an adult if they believe in God, some of them will say "I don't believe that God is an old man in heaven – but I think there exists 'something more'".

They think it is smarter to believe in "something more" than in "an old man in heaven".

Others can say "God is everything there is", or, "God is love". Since "something more", "everything there is", and "love" all exist – doesn't this mean that God exists?

This is cheating[2].

The cheating works like this: Imagine that you believe that ghosts don't exist, but that cars do. If someone then says that "Ghosts are cars", do you then all of a sudden believe that ghosts exist?

No, you don't. Ghosts are not cars. Ghosts are ghosts. And God is God, not "something else", "all there is", or "love".

Remember that, the next time you hear someone say "God is [whatever]".

---

[1]   The philosopher G.E. Moore described this way of cheating in his book *Principia Ethica.*

God as imaginary friend

Try to look at a star some clear night. You can choose whichever one you like. The light that hits your eye, the light that you see, has travelled through space thousands of years.

Now close your eyes.

The light that has travelled for thousands of years through space now instead hits our eyelid. There is no instrument or eye that registers that just that specific light has arrived.

Thousands of years travelling through space to land where it is not noticed.

Some people get a sense of vertigo when they have these kind of thoughts. Then perhaps they want someone to hold hands with; maybe a God, like an imaginary friend.

One can also believe in an imaginary friend so as to not have to feel alone.

But just because it feels good to pretend to hold a God's hand doesn't mean that gods exist.

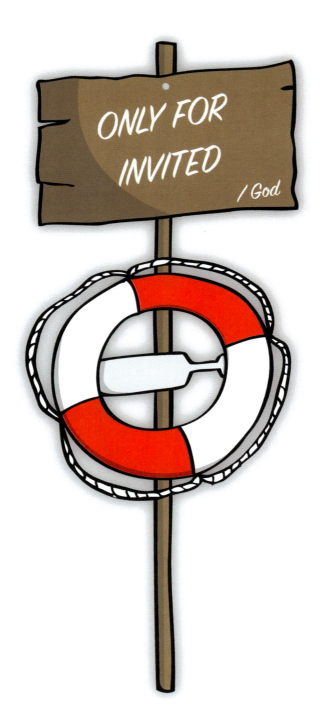

God as lifesaver

After natural disasters you often read about people who survived when many others died. Religious people sometimes say that God is good and can do everything. They say that he saved the survivors.

But if God was the lifesaver, why did he let all the other people die?

Why didn't he save everyone?

God as artist

"Look around. The world is so beautiful and perfect. Therefore God must exist!"

But everything in this world is not beautiful and perfect. Poor people are destitute, many people die for no good reason, and much is broken and ugly.

A God could have created the world much more beautiful and better – if he existed.

Christians and Muslims, for example, believe that there exists a heaven that is perfect which we come to when we die. So their God *can* create a perfect world.

So why do we need this world which is imperfect?

God as designer

Almost all religions have tales about how their God created everything. But if he did, their God is not much of a constructor, because people and animals are not particularly well designed.

Have you for example thought about why men have nipples? Women need them to give milk to their babies, but not men. It is just bad design.

We don't need our appendix either. And many people get back pains. This is bad design. Also, squid have much better eyes than we do.

Why did God make us like that? Doesn't he know how to make humans?[2]

---

[2] Charles Darwin discovered in the 1800s why we are constructed the way we are. His discovery of evolution is a much better explanation of these things than a clumsy God.

God as revelation

Some people claim that they have met Jesus. Or that they have seen miracles. Then surely God must exist?

But there are also people who claim that they *are* Jesus. Or that they have been kidnapped by space aliens. Why don't we believe them?

People can be mistaken, fantasize, or wish so strongly that they have seen something, that they remember things that have never happened. People can also lie, or be sick.

If you want to convince someone about something strange, it takes more than just stories. For example, that they get to see it for themselves.

But that is not how religions work. In religions you have to believe what others tell you.

God in the Bible and the Koran

"In the Bible and Koran it says that God exists. Then surely he must exist?"

But then you have to believe that the Bible or the Koran contains the truth in the first place.

How can you tell that some specific book is true? Just because the books themselves say that they are true?

If it were that simple it would be enough for me (the author of this book) to put a sticker on this book that says "TRUE".

That's a bit too easy, don't you think?

God for the smart?

"Many smart people believe in Gods. Then surely Gods must exist?"

But many smart people also believe that Gods do not exist. Does this then mean that Gods don't exist?

We can't find out if something is true by just investigating *who* believes in it. We also have to find out *why* they believe it.

Are there any good reasons to believe that Gods exists?

God as insurance

Some Gods promise a place in heaven to those who believe and a place in hell to those who don't believe. Doesn't that make it safest to believe in God?[3]

It doesn't seem very enjoyable to burn in hell for all eternity. And it is not a lot of work to believe that God exists.

But then you are left with the problem of what God to believe in. Many Gods send you to hell if you believe in the wrong God. And no one has found a way to tell which God is the right one to believe in.

Also, wouldn't a real God notice if you only pretended to believe because it is safest that way?

---

[3] This is called "Pascal's wager" because it was thought out by the French philosopher Blasie Pascal (1623–1662). It was easier in his time because he didn't have to mind any other religions than Christianity.

ZOROASTRIANS
ONLY
/GOD

God as the law

Some people claim that a God is needed to make people behave well. They think that people would steal and murder if there wasn't any threat of punishment after death.

That would mean that everyone who believes in, for example, the Bible or the Koran is good and everyone else evil. But that is not how it is.

If you know someone who believes that you have to believe in God to be good, then you should watch out. What if that person stops believing in God? Then that person can do anything.

If you look at people's behaviour it is pretty clear that no-one gets their ethics from the Bible or the Koran for real.

Because how many throw stones at their disobedient children? How many beat their slaves? Or give away all their belongings? Almost no one does these things, even though all of this is prescribed in the Bible.

Most people show good behaviour and are kind to each other in spite of all the strange rules in the Bible and the Koran.

God as comfort

Some people believe that bad things happen for a purpose. They say that it is "God's will" when someone dies or gets sick. People who reason like this think that it gives comfort to believe that God exists.

But what help is it to believe that God has a plan when a child gets sick or a puppy dies? Also, even if it would give comfort to believe in God, that doesn't mean that God exists.

It is false comfort to believe in Gods that don't exist. *Friends who give false comfort are false friends.*

Unfortunately, there isn't a meaning to everything that happens.

If something terrible happens to you, then try to remember that there still exists light, love and life in the world. These do not disappear, even when it feels that way.

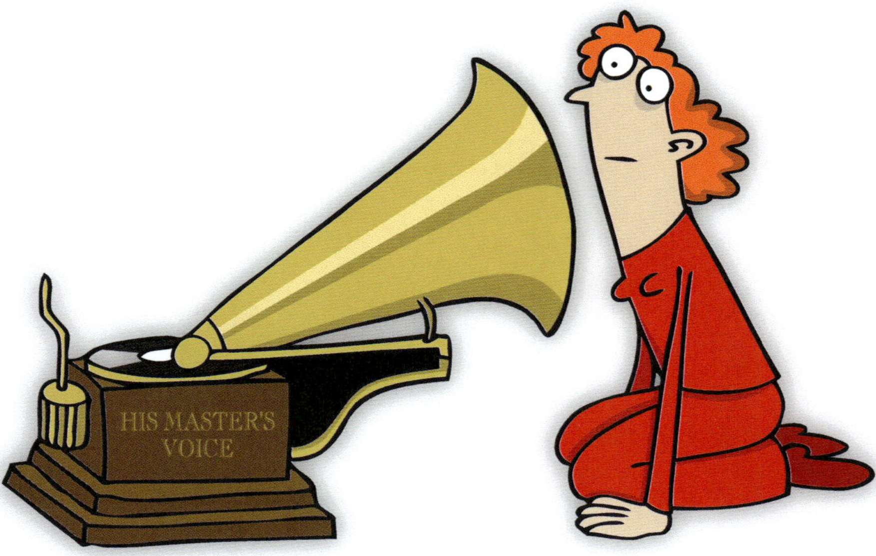
HIS MASTER'S
VOICE

God as the Meaning of Life

Why do so many people want to believe that there exists an outside force, a God, who gives meaning to life? Who wants to be a puppet or a robot that someone else controls?

Isn't it better to be free and to create your own Meaning of Life?

God as inspiration

Some people say that "Almost all beautiful things have been made by religious people. Books, art, architecture, music, many of the beautiful things in our world are inspired by God." And they are mostly right.

There is a lot of money in religion. Especially in the old days, the churches were among the richest. If you were a poor artist, musician, or architect, you often worked for the church. They paid well. Therefore a lot of art was created to honour the Gods.

Also, most people were religious in the old days. That is not something strange, because then we knew much less of how the world really works. And you risked being killed or banned if you said that you didn't believe in God.

Even if God worked fine as artistic inspiration, this proves nothing about his existence. There are those who find artistic inspiration in unicorns. But unicorns do not exist.

God as proven?

There are (really!) people who believe that God's existence can be proven like this:

"God is the most fantastic thing there is. It is more fantastic to exist that not to exist. Thus, God exists!"[4]

Then they think that they have magically proven existence by only using words. But if that is a valid argument, you can prove that God doesn't exist like this.

"God created everything. It is more fantastic to create everything without existing than if you exist. Thus, God doesn't exist!"

In reality, none of these proofs are valid. It is impossible to prove that God exists, but also impossible to prove that he doesn't.

That doesn't mean that it is equally probable that God exists as that he doesn't exist. (Read about Russell's teapot below.)

---

[4] This is called the ontological proof of God's existence. It is one of many attempts to prove God's existence that doesn't work.

Some reasons not to believe in Gods

Russell's teapot

Do you believe there is a teapot in orbit around the sun?[5] Most people don't. But how do they know that?

The answer is that we can't be sure that there exists no such teapot. Since no one can look everywhere at once, we can never be really sure that such a teapot doesn't exist.

But it would be really strange if such a teapot existed. On the other hand, it would be quite normal if such a teapot did not exist.

It is the same with Gods. We can't be totally sure that they don't exist. But if they had existed they could have zapped a big "WE EXIST" into a mountain side somewhere.

It would be very strange if Gods exist. But it would be quite normal if they don't.

---

[5] This thought experiment was invented by the philosopher Bertrand Russell (1872–1970). That is why it is called Russell's teapot.

Ethics isn't only about following rules

Ethics is the teaching of how one should behave; how to become a good human being.

Many religious people think that it is a good idea to follow God's commandments. They want to be able to stand before God and say "I did what you told me, I followed your rules".

But is that really good ethics? Doesn't this depend on which rules one follows?

In history we have seen several examples of when it has been bad to just follow rules. For example the people who followed Hitler and Stalin. They had the same answer as religious people about ethics. "I just followed the rules."

You shouldn't follow bad rules. (That's a good rule, don't you think?) The important thing is to look at the rules and think for yourself.

Some religious rules are immoral

In the Bible it says that you should stone your disobedient children[6]. From the stories about Muhammad you can learn that people who leave Islam should be beheaded. Surely, none of these rules should be obeyed? They are evil and oppressive.

But not all rules in the holy books are followed – not even by religious people themselves. This is not so strange, because even if some rules are good, other rules are very strange.

So how do religious people choose what rules to follow? Just like non-believers! They use common sense and listen to others.

In reality, almost no one gets their ethics from the holy books. That's why no one throws stones at disobedient children.

---

[6] Deuteronomy 21: 18–21

Ethics change

What is considered good ethics has changed during history.

Few people today think that there is something good in blindly following the orders of your superiors even if it leads to certain death. One hundred years ago, many did.

Slavery was once permitted. It says in several places in the bible that slavery is ok. Now we think that slavery is something horrendous.

We treat animals today pretty badly in our slaughter-houses. In the future animals may perhaps be treated better?

Ethics doesn't come from old books, but is something that has evolved over the history of mankind.

The holy books are too old

The Koran was written in the 600s by a man alone in a cave who thought he was listening to an angel. The Bible was written by a number of authors over hundreds of years, a long time ago. Some of the tales of Hinduism are so old that we don't have a really good sense of when they originated.

These books were written in a time when things we today find horrendous were part of daily life.

They contain old rules from a bygone era.

Many of these rules don't work today.

Slavery is always wrong

There are plenty of places in the Bible and the Koran where you can read about slavery. But it says nowhere that slavery is wrong.

The question about slavery is one of the simplest moral questions that ever has existed. Isn't it completely obvious that some people can't own others?

But there still is no prohibition of slavery in the holy books.

Many religious people have fought against slavery anyway. But these people fought slavery because they were good people. Not because they followed their holy books.

On the contrary, slave owners were able to cite many Bible verses in defense of slavery.

God's strange commandments

In the Bible, God wrote his Ten Commandments in stone. They are the only words that God wrote himself in the Bible, so they must be particularly important. (Why didn't he write it all?)

The first commandments are of course about God himself. About Him being the Only God.

Then there follows some simple rules that are the same in almost all ethical systems (not to kill, commit adultery, steal, or lie).

Then follows one commandment that forbids wrongful *thinking* (not to want someone else's house, wife, slave, ox or ass, or anything else).

But there are no commandments against child abuse, rape, or slavery.

For the Christian God it is more important that you do not worship Thor than that you do not abuse children, or rape, or use others as slaves.

Non-believers are neither good nor bad

There have existed – and still exist – many evil people in the world. Some of these evil people have been – and are – non-believers.

Stalin almost certainly did not believe in a God. Hitler almost certainly did (although some people claim the opposite). They are two of History's worst mass murderers. But even if both didn't believe in Gods, they did not murder *because* they were non-believers.

Hitler and Stalin both had a moustache. But none of them murdered *because* they had a moustache.

You do not become an evil person from not believing in God, or from being religious, or from having a moustache. Neither do you become a good person from not believing in God, or from being religious, or from having a moustache.

To be a non-believer only means that you do not believe that Gods exist.

Don't just believe what others say

The problems with Hitler's and Stalin's teachings were that they were too much like religions. They both contain things you have to believe even if reality says something else.

It is important to think for yourself. This is not only true for religions, but for politics and everything else.

Don't believe anything that you don't have a good reason to believe!

There is no society on earth where people have suffered because the people in power have been too wise or too reasonable.

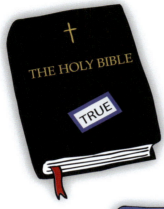

Is evil the result of free will?

If God can do what he wants and is benevolent at the same time, then why is there evil and suffering in the world?[7] How can God let a little innocent puppy get run over by a car? Or look on without doing anything when the strong bully the weak?

One attempt at an answer is this: God created people with free will. So it is our own poor choices that make the world evil. It is our own fault that evil exists.

But it is hardly the run-over puppy's own fault that he is dead? Or a small child's who becomes ill?

---

[7] In philosophy, this is called the theodicy-problem. People have thought about it for centuries. Non-belief has solved it. If there are no Gods then there is no philosophical problem.

Does evil exist because we don't understand God's will?

Another attempt at explaining why evil exists is to say that "Maybe we just don't understand what God wants? Maybe it just *seems* evil but is really good?" But to say that in connection with sick children and run-over puppies is not much of an explanation.

Also, if we can't understand what God is doing, how can we hope to understand what he wants us to do?

Maybe God can't do what he wants? Maybe he isn't good? These two answers do seem to work. But they certainly take away some of God's shine.

(Some people have solved the problem of evil by believing in many gods: some good, some bad. And then the problem goes away. But that doesn't mean that there exist many Gods. It only means that some religions have smarter solutions for some problems than do others.)

Is eternal life the solution?

Some say that the solution to the problem of the existence of evil and suffering is eternal life. If we live forever – as it says in the holy books – then maybe everything turns out alright in the end anyway?

But if God has created a perfect world where we end up when we die, why couldn't we get there from the beginning? What is the point of letting some people suffer before they can come to heaven?

And what is the point of letting people burn in hell for all eternity? If God has created all people and knows everything, then why does he create someone who will have to suffer for eternity? For the people who end up in hell, eternal life must be more of a problem than a solution.

Why does evil exist? Epicurus' answer

A Greek philosopher[8] long ago summarized the problem with God, suffering and evil in this way:

"Is God willing to prevent evil, but not able? Then he is impotent.

Is he able, but not willing? Then he is malevolent.

Is he both able and willing? Then where does suffering and evil come from?

Is he neither able nor willing? Then why call him God?"

---

[8] Epicurus (341–270 BCE)

You don't choose for yourself what Gods to believe in

Most believers have received their faith in God from their parents and through their culture. No one goes through all the different Gods that have been invented, reads about, for example, the flying spaghetti monster on the internet and says "No. I do not believe in *that* God.". There exist, and have existed, so many Gods that it is impossible to read about them all.

Most parents tell their children that ghosts don't exist. Some religious parents, on the other hand, tell their children that God exists. Some religious parents also tell their children that they will burn in hell for all eternity if they don't believe in the God they tell them about.

But it is equally improbable that ghosts exist as that God exists. And isn't it cruel to scare your children that they will burn in hell forever?

If God exists, isn't it enough that children will learn about it when they are old enough to think for themselves? If the parents' beliefs are so much better than everyone else's, then why do parents have to scare their children when they are small and helpless?

Closed for
Sabbath

Why do people pray?

Some people believe that God determines what has happened and what will happen. Even so, they ask him for help in their prayers.

But if their God knows everything, then he already knows what he will do. Then he can't change his mind.

So why do people pray?

(Strangely, most Christians pray on Sundays, the day their Lord has set aside for rest.)

God can't do everything

Some people believe that God can do everything. But can he make a rock that is so heavy that he can't lift it? Or a riddle that is so tricky that he can't figure out the solution?

If he can do the former, then he can't do the latter. Surely, God can make $2 + 2 = 5$?

If you ask these types of questions to someone who believes in God, then they will say that they are old and childish questions. This is true. The problem is that no one has answered them yet.

"My God can do what he wants!" Yes, of course a made-up God can do what he wants. But if you believe that Gods can do everything, then these types of unsolvable problems come up.

Some people answer by saying that "God does not exist in this world, but outside it." Then abracadabra they think that the problem is gone. Now, that is a really childish answer.

But about a made-up God you can of course make up anything you like.

Watch out!

Most religions have ideas about reality. Sometimes these ideas agree with how reality really is, but sometimes they don't.

In the Bible it says that life, the universe, and everything was created in six days. Today we know that it took almost 14 billion years.

Either you believe in the holy books, but have to shut your eyes to reality. Or you believe in reality, but have to shut your eyes to what it says in the holy books.

To be religious is therefore to choose to shut your eyes. Either to reality because of what it says in the holy books, or to the holy books because reality says something else.

It is not good to shut your eyes. Isn't it better to meet reality with your eyes open?

All holy books can't be true

Some people have the opinion that you shouldn't say that any of the holy books were created by people.

But there are many holy books that are claimed to come from, or have been inspired by, God. The problem is that different things are said in each of these holy books. Among other things, they say that the other holy books have it wrong.

To say that most holy books are mistaken is therefore to state the obvious. It has to be true; it says so in the books themselves!

It is never good to believe that made-up things actually are true

When we go to school we learn to tell the difference between true and false. We learn that the earth is round, and not flat. We learn that the universe wasn't created in six days, but came to be over a very long time.

Religion is the only field where it is not allowed to say "But that can't be true!"

Why should one area have its own rules for how and what should be allowed to be thought? Why should religion have its own area where errors can stand unchallenged?

Don't religions take themselves seriously?

Reality is more exciting than fairy-tales

In some holy books it says that the universe is 6 000 years old, that the earth was created in six days, or that the earth rests on a turtle's back.

We know today that there are billions of galaxies. That time moves at different speeds depending on your velocity! We have begun to understand how life originated and functions. The world that has been revealed through science can sometimes be hard to understand, but it is amazing.

In comparison to reality, the world-view of religions is so meagre that it hardly deserves to count as a world-view at all.

Why religion sometimes is dangerous

Violence in the name of religion

Throughout history, there has been much violence in the name of Gods. And, of course, some non-believers have also done evil things.

People do good and evil deeds whether or not they believe in gods.

The strange thing is that some people seem to think that you become a better person if you believe in a God. But if that was true, there shouldn't be any religious violence.

But there is. A lot.

People with different religions have wars with each other in many places around the world. In other places, wars are carried out *within* the same religion about different ways of being a "true" Christian, or a "true" Muslim. Men lock their wives and daughters in their houses, parents cut away pieces of their children's genitalia, people blow themselves and others into pieces. Everything for their God.

There are many causes of violence. Religion, that claims to make people better, is one of them.

All causes of violence are bad and dangerous.

It can be dangerous to believe in a reward in heaven

Most people who would sit down at the controls of a large passenger plane would do their utmost to avoid crashing.

A person who wilfully would try to hit a building filled with even more unknown people would be mad.

But there can be another explanation – the person may believe in a reward in heaven.

It is lethally dangerous to make people believe in a reward in heaven. Especially if that reward comes after killing in the name of God.

Religious ethics increase suffering

Ethics is the teaching of how to behave. It poses questions such as "What is right and wrong?" and "What is good and evil?"

Right and good should be things such as being kind, helpful, thoughtful, caring and so on; behaviours that decrease suffering in the world.

Many Catholic priests and Muslim imams instead think that an important moral rule is not to use condoms.

But condoms protect against deadly diseases such as Aids. Thus, such a rule condemns many people to a painful death and many children to growing up as orphans.

Everyone knows this, but in spite of this the priests and imams think that it is more important how adults behave in the privacy of their own bedrooms than to prevent fatal diseases.

This is one of many examples of religious ethics not being about reducing suffering in the world. Instead, it is about following rules and obeying orders. Sometimes the rules are good, but often they are not.

Last words

If there is a God we should listen!

If God exists and has left a message in a book, then we should really listen, read the book, and do what it says.

But if God does not exist and all the holy books are written by people, then we shouldn't have those books as the basis for anything. Then they are just ordinary books.

There is no middle ground. How can one believe that there are books that come from God, but that we don't have to care about what they say? Or that there are books that do not come from God, but that we have to follow their strange rules anyway?

If the holy books are made up by ordinary people, then they shouldn't have any more influence on our lives than any other books. There are many books with more colourful tales, better ethics, more beautiful language, and a more comforting content.

Which books are important for you are best determined by yourself.

Fundamentalist non-belief

Those who call non-believers "fundamentalists" assume that the non-believers are so sure of themselves that they want to ban religion. But that is not so. Everyone has the right to believe what they want to.

Some people think that religions should be left alone. They think that non-believers who point out all the errors and contradictions in religions are fundamentalists. They want religions to be a separate collection of thoughts that no one should be allowed to question.

Of course, that would be convenient for them!

For the people who think that it is fundamentalist and intolerant to criticize religion this book can be summarized in one sentence:

Don't believe anything that you don't have a good reason to believe!

That's about as fundamentalist as it gets.

Gods and society

Not even people who believe in Gods can explain how we are to know which religion is the right religion. When they say "*Our* God is the only God, *their* God doesn't exist" they use the same arguments against the existence of other gods as are used in this book to argue that *no* gods exist.

What does that mean for society? How much should religion be allowed to influence our lives?

Non-believers obviously do not want to be influenced by other peoples' religion. Why should anything be forced upon you that you don't believe?

But it is actually the same for believers. What Christian wants to live under Islamic law? What Muslim wants to attend end-of-school ceremonies at the local Hindu temple and eat food that first has been sanctified by an idol?

There is only one way to make sure that no one's religion is forced upon others. Government and religion have to be kept separate.

Religion is something that every person has the right to choose themselves – or reject.

Not to believe is to be free!

If you say "no" to Gods you say "yes" to other things at the same time. Because to not believe is to be free!

Not free to hurt other people or to do what you want. Such freedom would violate the freedom of others.

But free from others' made-up super beings.

Free from others' invented eternal punishments.

Free to think what you like.

Free from feeling bad for eating the "wrong" food or loving the "wrong" person.

Not to believe is to understand that we humans only have each other. That is fantastic enough!

Thanks!

I would like to thank Christer Sturmark, Eva Ortmark, Anna Blixt, Ulf Lindholm, Pia Fagerström, Johan Lind, Magnus Enquist and Pontus Strimling for help and commentary. Also, special thanks to Ellis Wohlner and Cynthia Scott-Clark for assistance with the English language. But most of all I would like to thank my beloved Anna, for inspiration and help with the text, but above all for being my life companion – what an adventure we are living! Thanks also to my children for all the happiness that you give.

I am also grateful to Richard Dawkins, Sam Harris, Christopher Hitchens and many of my friends for ideas. Most arguments in this book are not my own, but have been used by others throughout history. As a collator and summarizer I am therefore indebted to many previous authors.

Other books about not believing in Gods

Richard Dawkins: "The God Delusion" (2006),
Bantam Press.

Sam Harris: "Letter to a Christian Nation" (2006),
Alfred A. Knopf.

Christopher Hitchens: "God is Not Great" (2007),
Atlantic books.

Christopher Hitchens: "The Portable Atheist" (2007),
Da Capo Press.

Michael Onfray: "The Atheist Manifesto" (2007),
Arcade Publishing.

Printed in Great
Britain
by Amazon